From A to Zamboni®

The Alphabet, Rangers® Style!

Written by

Jennifer Grocki

Illustrated by

Andy Lendway

From A to Zamboni
The Alphabet, Rangers Style!

Copyright © 2013 by Jennifer Grocki

Illustrations Copyright © 2013 by Andy Lendway

All Rights Reserved

Team Kidz Inc.

P.O. Box 2111

Voorhees, NJ 08043

ISBN 10: 097938334X

ISBN 13: 978-0-9793833-4-2

Dedication

In loving memory of my mother Judy, who had a passion for life,
literature, and hockey, and to my niece Lilly and nephew Jack
in hopes that they follow in her footsteps.

- JG

This one is for Tom, Yan, Tommy and Frank. The best Ranger fans I know!

- AL

A is for Anthem, we sing with great pride,

B is for Bench, where we sit side by side.

C is for Coach, who stands tall and proud,

D is for Defense, through which no goal's allowed.

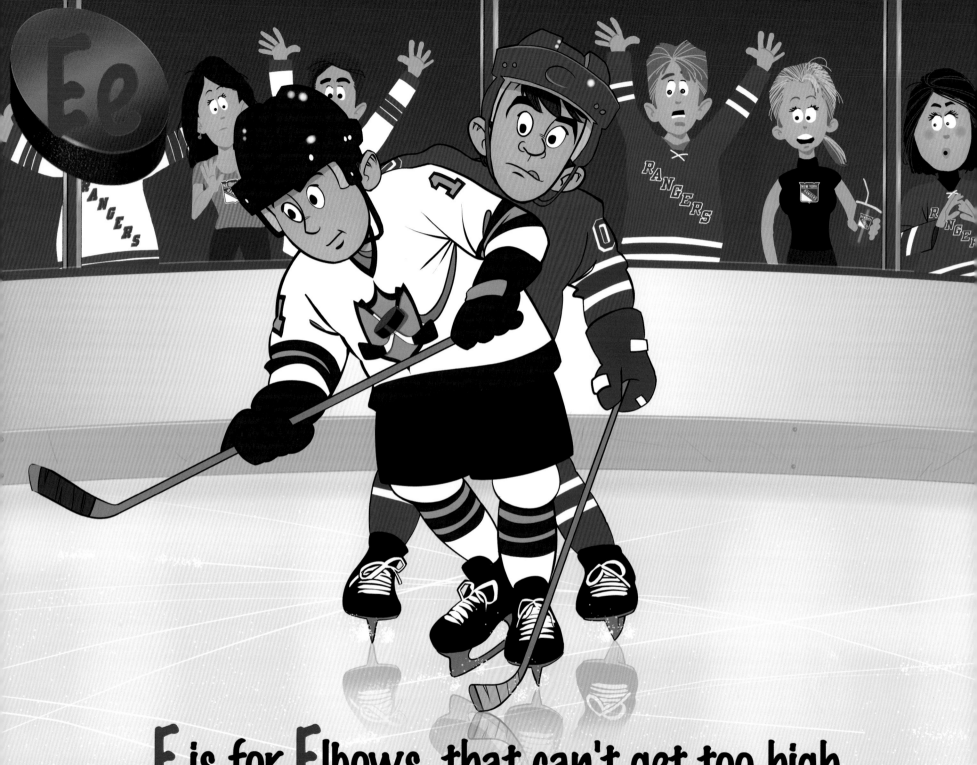

E is for Elbows, that can't get too high,

F is for Fans, who watch us fly by.

G is for Goalie, who guards our team's net,

H is for Hat Trick, we'll never forget!

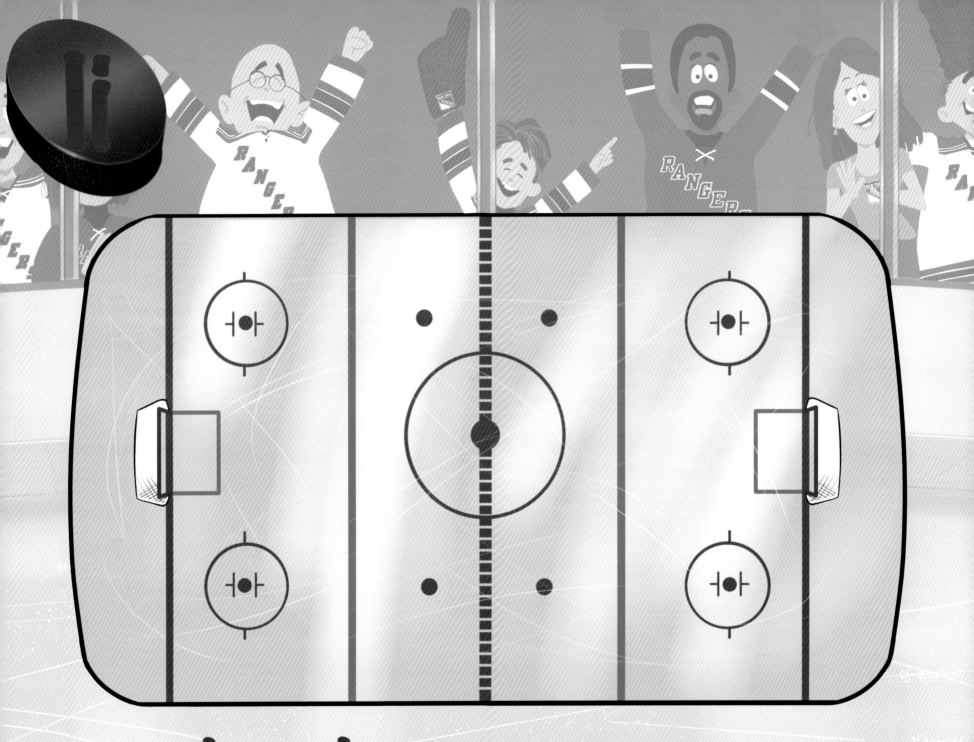

I is for Ice, we can't play without,

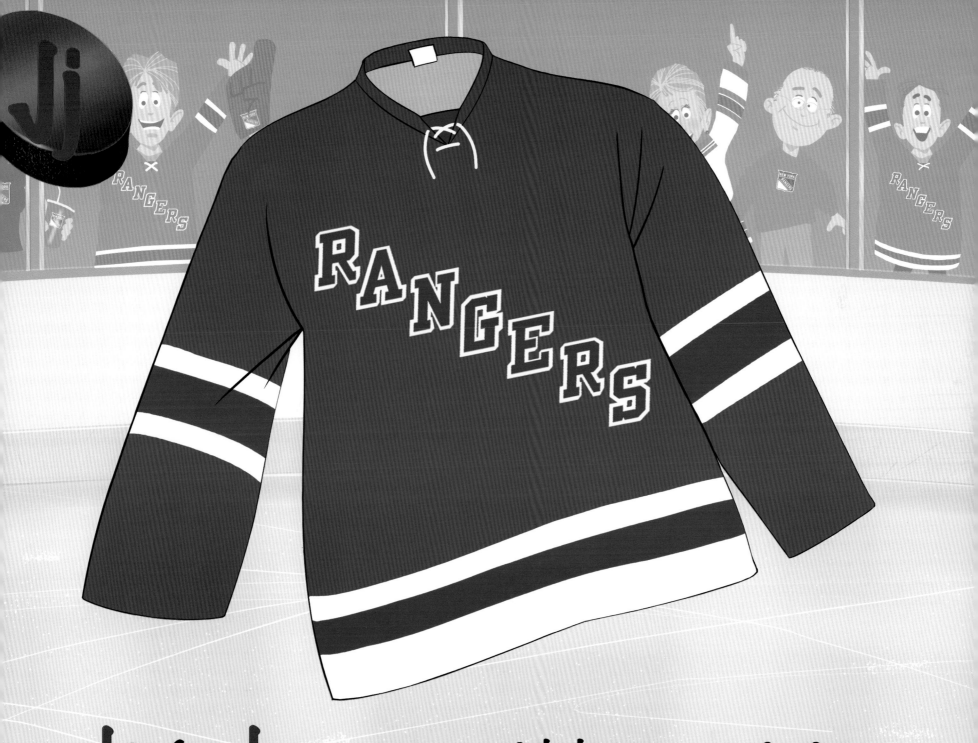

J is for Jersey, worn with honor, no doubt.

K is for Kicking, we know we can't do,

L is for Linesman, whose eyes are on you.

M is for Mask, which we wear on our face,

N is for Net, where the puck finds its place.

O is for Obstruction, which gets you the door,

P is for Puck, we pass, shoot, and we score!

Q is for Quiet, when we don't have the lead,

R is for Red Line, we cross with great speed.

S is for **S**tick, we handle with care,

T is for Team, who will always be there.

U is for Underdog, which we've all been before,

V is for **V**ictory, the moment we score!

W is for **W**inger, who passes just right,

X is for **X**s, used to plan for game night.

Y is for **Y**ippee, you yell with a friend,

Z is for **Z**amboni® machine, making ice at **The End!**

Autographs

Autographs